the

Due [Dü]
Season

Marina Angelica Coryat

This book is dedicated to my parents, Ruben and Pearl Coryat,

Texas State Representative Senfronia Thompson,

Apostle John Eckhardt

and

those who are waiting on the promises of God

to be manifested in their lives on

earth as it is in heaven.

Table of Contents

Foreword

There are moments in one's life that you feel humbled or a sense of awe. This is one of those moments for me. Moreover, I have been privileged to write a comment regarding some literary work but I have never been asked to pen a foreword to a book. Of course, I readily agreed to do a foreword for the author. In fact, I was more than honored to have been asked after getting over the original shock.

The author, Marina Coryat, and I met over 20 years ago. However, we bumped into each other on the political and sometimes activist circuit. It is those fundamental issues that seem to draw certain like-minded people together. Issues that most Americans take for granted while others spend sometimes a life trying to convince others that the right that they have and enjoy should be available to all. Marina has been politically involved for many years, and thank God she has been on the right side of the issues.

Now, I would like to share with you a bit more about her. Marina is the oldest of five children born to an Indian mother and a Black father from the country of Trinidad. She speaks several languages- Japanese, Spanish and some Kiswahili. I have admired her for this intelligence as one of the communications directors of the City of Houston. She was very effective and proficient in her job.

However, she decided to venture out into her own business, after gaining private sector experience. That is another quality I admire in her; she has a gentle boldness and a deep sense of dedication about her. In addition, honesty and integrity are worn about her as garlands around her neck. It is surprising to find persons within her age group who have a high regard for humanity and an awesome regard for Almighty God.

I took Marina with me to Chile one year because of her ability to speak Spanish. We did some site visits with a group when we were there. One of the places that we visited was a camp where many Chilean people had been tortured and died. I knew she felt sad for the people after visiting. We could feel the dark presence even though it had been many years since any activity had taken place there. While we were there for several days, Marina was isolated from me during the day because of the meetings that I had to attend. One day after spending hours in a meeting, I felt badly for Marina being alone to discover Marina was witnessing to the Chilean people and even thought of laying hands on them. When I heard this, I wondered if she knew the dominant religion there was Catholic; but I recalled Marina was once Catholic. Meanwhile, I did give her a bit of caution only to learn the next day she had gone over to the city ministering. I quickly dismissed my fears and left her in the hands of the Holy Spirit. My prayer was to get back to the United States safely and bring Marina back in one piece. Needless to say, God answered my prayer.

So her embarkment into the prophetic is no surprise to me. Since her conversion from being a quiet Catholic to being a fiery spirit-filled Christian, she has devoted volumes of time daily feasting upon God's Word. She also served faithfully as an adjutant to her Pastor who flows in the prophetic. She graduated from the School of the Prophets, Kingdom School of Ministry and keeps her gifts stirred up with Impact University and other webinars. Occasionally, she drags me to hear someone new to the city of Houston to minister in a particular phase of God's Word. One thing I can say from the outset, she is not fake and reveres God's Word and the Holy Trinity.

When I read her book, the Due [Du] Season which contained the prophetic impartation, I recalled bits and pieces she had been sharing with me verbally. At first, I thought it was a small prophecy, but as she began to release it in the book, I knew it was an authentic prophecy and a prophetic Word that needed to be recognized.

I went over the prophetic Word again and began to ponder. Is this an evaluation of conduct: God's people too caught up in materialism-money making, greed, disregard of mankind, pleasure and faith misplaced? It became somewhat frightening to reread the prophetic Word, but there was enlightenment and encouragement to those God is ready to release the answers to their long awaited prayers. In addition, there is a requirement for Due, Dew, Do and Deux of each of us. Also, the awakening to God evaluation and His release to long awaited answers to prayers all hinges upon us.

I want to encourage you to get the book and read it twice. Most of all, meditate on the scriptures Marina listed after each section. Believe me, she does the meditation daily as well as periodic fasting, while I am still trying to fit all these things in.

In the end, you and I know this truth. God gives to each a task He wants us to fulfill. It does not matter where we live, the car we drive, the long hours we work. What is going to matter is did we do it to the glory of Him. Did we love those who seem unlovable, feed the hungry...treat our neighbor as ourselves and most of all forgive the person(s) we felt do not deserve forgiveness.

I invite you to read the book, *The Due [Dü] Season* and discover what awaits you.

Senfronia Thompson
Texas State Representative

Endorsements

After our New Year's Eve service, Minister Marina Coryat, shared with me that the Lord had given her a Word for 2020 and beyond. She told me: "The Lord said it was Due, Dew, and Do time and season." I asked her to share the Word of the Lord with my church on the next Sunday. I knew that there was oil on that word. For her, she was fine with just releasing it to me, but I knew that this was a corporate word that needed to reach the Body of Christ. I am so honored that this powerful and timely Word of God was first released in our house.

The Due [Dü] Season is indeed a Word from the Lord for those who feel down trodden through the perils of life. Our church was reinvigorated by this fresh word and the impartation that came from this mighty vessel of God. Ever since the time that this revelatory word was delivered, I have seen evidence in my life, the church, country, and earth that is demonstrative of this God-breathed word. When you read this prophetic book, you will find yourself resuscitated because you will know and see manifestations of your Due, Dew and Do Season come forth.

Apostle Tony Ervin
God Encounter Church

In the book, *The Due (Dü) Season,* Prophetess Marina Coryat expounds and elucidates the unique trio of Due, Dew and Do prophetically and practically. After reading this book, we personally began to receive everything that was overdue because the due season had come. We can talk all day about the impact of this awesome book. Well done, Prophetess and Philanthropist Marina for a life-transforming read.

Pastors C. Kuda & N. Grace Kapswara
New Life Covenant Church under
Bishop Tudor and Pastor ChiChi Bismark
"Is There Anything Too Hard for the Lord?"

I celebrate my sister in love, Prophetess Marina Angelica Coryat on the completion of her first book, *The Due (Dü) Season.* In seasons of crisis and disruption, God always speaks though his prophets to send words of comfort, encouragement, and edification for His people. As you read this book, my prayer is that the dew of heaven reigns over your life, your due surprise manifests suddenly, and you accomplish all that you set out to do. May the Lord give you double "deux" for your trouble.

Minister Mellonie Baldwin, The Achor Collective

Min. Marina Coryat has been such a great inspiration to many. You can always see the love of Jesus she holds in her heart. I witnessed her initial message when she received her license into the ministry. I have watched God perform many miracles, signs, and wonders in her life. Watch out, God is not finished with you yet. This fantastic book, The Due (Dü) Season will stir your gifts and activate the word of God in your heart. It is filled with prophetic insight that will challenge you to believe God for more in your life. This is an awesome read to ignite the fire of God in your life. I pray that everyone who reads this book will began to soar in the fullness of God. It is your Due (Dü) Season. It is your birthing season now! It is time to receive your double portion.

Prophetess Debra Reagans
Founding Director, Prophetic
Empowerment International Ministries

Acknowledgements

To my beautiful sisters (listed alphabetically), Minister Marcia Bazile, Ashley Brooks, Andrea Davis, Deavra Daughtery, Felicia Davis, Sharon Jenkins, Mayra Hypolite, Marcia Menefield, Stephanie Thomas, Belinda Wiggins, and Pamela Williams, thank you for your listening ears, friendship, love, and support with this book and life.

I thank God for friends and leaders in ministry who trust the God in me and push me to higher heights (listed alphabetically):

Mrs. Jeanette Allen, Dr. Shirene Anderson, Pastor Ray Bady, Minister Mellonie Baldwin, Pastor Linda Callaway, Pastor Craig Barnett, Apostle LaJun Cole, Prophetess Valora Cole, Prophet John Deland Coleman, Pastor Glenn Davis, Prophetess Bettie Davis, Pastor Augustine Degorl, Minister Ralphena Dodson, Apostle Tony Ervin, Prophetess Rebecca Fells, Pastor Deborah Ford, Apostle Stephen

Garner, Pastor Mark Grafenreed, Apostle Travis Jennings, Dr. Otis Johnson, Pastors Kuda and Grace Kapswara, Prophetess Michelle J. Miller, Prophetess Kendria Moore, Pastor Kim Orr, Prophetess Debra Reagans, Pastor Kissuth Reamo, Apostle Marcus Rivers, Bishop Terri Smith, Pastor Lovie Sophus, Dr. Cindy Trimm, Prophetess Michelle Wilburn, Apostle John Veal, Pastor Victoria Wells, Apostle Wanda Wiltz, and Prophet Tommy Wiltz.

I am grateful for my local pastors, Pastors Kirbyjon and Suzette Caldwell for their covering and for providing a place of great healing after a great devastation in my life years ago. It has been an honor to serve with my Windsor Village Church Family.

Words cannot express my appreciation to my Apostle John Eckhardt, who God used to resuscitate me back into ministry and into the prophetic. Along with Apostle Eckhardt falls the IMPACT Network of so many loved ones who share and coach me along the way. Thank you!

Thank you to my Executive Board of SunArise International Ministries and volunteers for trusting the God in me and moving as He desires. Without you, the Prayer, Praise and Pursuit Gatherings would not have been birthed to full term. It was the catalyst to writing my first book.

None of this would have been birthed without the best parents in the world, Ruben, and Pearl Coryat. I thank you for your demonstration of unconditional love. To my siblings,

Joseph, Peter, Blossom, and Ronald, although we differ in many ways, I love you and there is nothing you can do about it.

Now the time is past due. Let me begin sharing the Word the Lord has given me.

Introduction

I inquired of the Lord: "What is the Word of the Lord for 2020 and beyond?"

The Holy Spirit responded to me: "Due, dew, and do time." In English, these three words have the same phonetic sound but different spellings.

So, New Year's Eve 2019, I drove to a friend's church called "God Encounters." I got there at midnight. At that point, many prophetic declarations were already given by the ministers. I did not want to be out of order, so after the service, I spoke with Apostle Tony Ervin and shared that the Lord had given me a word for the New Year for 2020 and season.

I shared that beginning 2020 was the year of DUE, DEW, and DO. He responded, "There is oil on that" and said that they were still receiving what the Lord had to say. He then invited me to deliver the word on the first Sunday of January 2020.

In this book is the prophetic word that was delivered that day. Since that time, the Lord has added more understanding and content to this word. In 2 Chronicles 20:20, the Word says, "Believe in the Lord your God, so shall ye be established; believe his prophets, so shall ye prosper."

Many are wondering what is happening in this chaotic world. Individuals may ask, "What about my promises from God? When is my *due* season? How much longer, Lord?"

Galatians 6:9 says, "And let us not be weary in well doing: for in *due* season we shall reap if we faint not."

As you read this book, *The Due (Dü) Season*, you will be encouraged to know that your days of waiting are soon to be over. The promises have already begun to manifest. Romans 8:19 says the whole earth is groaning (travailing) for the "manifestation of the sons of God." You are in your birthing season, so know that the groans, pain, and uncomfortableness of this time will soon give way to the biggest blessings you could ever imagine.

Read on to be encouraged by the Word and how God expounds through revelation. In this book, you will get inspiration, instructions, and impartation. There are also prayers and declarations for you to bombard heaven as you stake your claim on the Due Season.

I am so excited to hear the testimonies that have already begun to happen since this word was delivered at the beginning of 2020. With the turning of each page and as you read, you will be transported into your Dü season. Your eyes have not seen nor have your ears heard what God is going to do. Without further ado, I present to you that which we have been waiting for, *The Due (Dü) Season.*

THE DUE (DU) SEASON

The Word given to Marina A. Coryat on 12/31/2019

This word was delivered publicly by Marina A. Coryat on 1/5/2020 at God Encounters Church in Houston, Texas

The Lord said that this is the "Due Time, the Dew Time, and the Do Time." In English, these three words have the same phonetic sound but different spellings. These words are considered homonyms to each other. This is significant, but before I delve into this, let's hear what the Lord said about DUE, then DEW, then DO!

DUE

"The year 2020 begins DUE Time," the Lord declared. "Just as a bill or a project is due, so it is an appointed time for you. As a mother is to give birth, there is a set time or a due date. Many things seemed as if they would never come, but I have set this as your DUE Time. Many have things that are owed to them. Many things seem as though they are overdue. Trust me in knowing that I make all things beautiful in my time," the Lord reassured. *"There are things that*

are due to you that you do not even remember. Yes, there is a set time to favor Zion, and it is now. Many have become frustrated even as of recent but know that DUE time is here. For I am birthing that which is in you. As those dreams, projects, and desires come to pass, do not forget to give me the honor to which I am due. As you render honor unto me, you will even see that honor will be bestowed upon you. Yes, I'm calling forth your DUE Time, due season, due portions, and due order to come. This has come after your due diligence and honor. For many of you have toiled in the field, and it is DUE Time for your crop to harvest. This begins the year of the DUE. This is also the year of the DEW."

DEW

"When does the dew come?" the Lord asked. "The dew comes at night before the day," He explained. 'Weeping may endure for a night but joy comes in the morning,' He reminded. I will bring this dew to you as a sign and a wonder. Even as the Israelites complained in the past, so have many of you, yet I still provided for all of you in the wilderness. I continue to make manna from dew. You will taste and see heavenly blessings in this year. Things that cannot be explained, but I will hasten my word to perform it. For yes, the DUE Time and the DEW Time are here."

The Lord said, *"This will be a year of dew. There will be tangible moisture that will be made manifest. The dew is a sign. I am going to demonstrate through the weather and other supernatural occurrences. I will do creative miracles just as with the creation of manna from the dew."*

DO

The Lord said, *"This is the time to DO. It is time to just do it. There are things that you have put on the back burner. There will be time to do hobbies and things you said that you never had time to do. Do it. I am calling you to do what I called you to do. Even as Deuteronomy talks about the dos. I'm calling you to be a "do-it-er on me." The book gives you to do and not to do. I tell you what not to do. This is not a time to do what is wrong or rather disobey. Obedience is better than sacrifice. Do what I called you to do. In Deuteronomy 28, I tell you what to do and not to do. Also remember My Word in Deuteronomy 8:18 where I give you the power to get wealth."*

DEUX

As I was studying the scriptures with dew, due, and do, the Lord said, *"There is another 'do'."* *"I asked him, "What "do"? He continued patiently speaking to me with an accented "do". With emphasis, I asked again. "Do?" He confirmed, "Yes, do". There is a French word which is a "do". So, I looked it up, and there it was "DEUX". Deux is the number two. The Lord shared that this is the year 2020. "Twenty (20) is redemption and even in the fullness of time, I have come," he explained. "I will give you a double redemption.*

I will restore to you that which the locust, cankerworm, and palmerworm have taken from you. Two is the number of witnesses. There will be greater evangelism." Then, the Lord advised, *"Go forth, especially in twos, to do greater evangelism. Some have begun to say that 2020 is the year of vision, but it is also 5780 (Hebraic calendar) which is of the mouth. You must speak. One can bring a thousand to flight but two can bring 10,000 to flight. It will take at least two to participate – one to speak and one to listen. Two (2) means double. Double blessings. As I spoke in James 5:7, I want you to be patient, for the early and latter rain are coming. That's two (2), the DEUX!"*

This begins your season of DUE, DEW, DO, and DEUX.

DUE

DUE

"The year 2020 begins DUE Time," the Lord declares. "Just as a bill or a project is due, so it is an appointed time for you. As a mother is to give birth, there is a set time or a due date. Many things seemed as if it would never come, but I have set this as your DUE Time. Many have things that are owed to them. Many things seem as though they are over-due. Trust me in knowing that I make all things beautiful in my time," the Lord reassures. *"There are things that are due to you that you do not even remember. Yes, there is a "set time to favor Zion, and it is now. Many have become frus-trated even as of recent but know that DUE Time is here. For I am birthing that which is in you. As those dreams, proj-ects, and desires come to pass, do not forget to give me the honor to which I am due. As you render honor unto me, you will even see that honor will be bestowed upon you. Yes, I'm calling forth your DUE Time, due season, due portions, and due order to come. This has come after your due diligence and honor. For many of you have toiled in the field, and it is DUE Time for your crop to harvest. This begins the year of the DUE."*

This is what the Lord spoke to me. I don't know about you, but for me, this was a super word of the Lord to hear. It res-onated in my Spirit. It resonated with those who heard the word that was released on the first Sunday of January 2020.

As reflect on that word, I know that this will come to pass on a greater dimension. Late in January 2020, I received a call from my ex-husband. I did not even recognize his voice. He called me to ask for my address and said that the reason he was calling was a good thing. He was sending me a check for the money from our divorce decree. That was seven years ago. This was such a surprise to me to receive the call, and then two days later, I received the check. Some things are *due* to you that you may have even forgotten or written off. I honestly believe that just like me with this example, we will see more manifestations of things that were *due* to us come to the surface and be a blessing in this *due* season.

One of the ladies in our ministry received a class action lawsuit check in January 2020 that she did not even file for. She does not know how her name got on the list, but God does. God is behind the scenes lining things up for His children. Money that was *due* to her without her knowledge came to fruition.

These are only a couple of examples, but we know that His word does not lie. We will see more financial blessings come into our hands beginning this year. There will be surprises. There will be gifts and other honorariums that will land in your hands. I heard the Lord saying, "These blessings will be bestowed upon you. Hidden treasures." He reminded me of Isaiah 45:1-3 NLT which is below. Read it aloud and make it personal. Where you see Cyrus' name, put your name there.

¹ "This is what the Lord says to Cyrus, his anointed one, whose right hand he will empower. Before him, mighty kings will be paralyzed with fear. Their fortress gates will be opened, never to shut again.

² This is what the Lord says: "I will go before you, Cyrus, and level the mountains. I will smash down gates of bronze and cut through bars of iron.

³ And I will give you treasures hidden in the darkness—secret riches. I will do this so you may know that I am the Lord, the God of Israel, the one who calls you by name" (Isaiah 45:1-3 New Living Translation Bible).

The Greek word for "*due*" is "idios." It means "one's own" or "distinct" or "personal." The Greek for "season" is "Kairos" which can mean a number of things, but specifically, here it can mean "a suitable time or favorable moment or opportunity where you can take advantage of things coming to a head."

This is indeed a time for us to take advantage of this favorable season – not only for this year, but for coming years. This is our *Due* Time!

DUE Scriptures for Mediation

1 Peter 5:6-7. KJV

> 6 "Humble yourselves therefore under the mighty hand of God, that he may exalt you in *due* time:
>
> 7 Casting all your cares upon him; for he careth for you."

Galatians 6:9. KJV

> "And let us not be weary in well doing: for in *due* season we will reap; if we fail not."

Psalms 104:27

> "These all wait for you; that thou mayest give them meat in *due* season."

Psalms 145:15

> "The eyes of all wait upon thee; and you give them their meat in *due* season."

Romans 5:6 KJV

> "When we yet without strength, in *due* time Christ died for the ungodly."

Romans 5:6 AMP

"While we were still helpless (powerless to provide for our salvation) at the right time Christ died (as a substitute) for the ungodly."

Romans 13:7

"Render therefore to all their *dues*: tribute to whom tribute is *due*; custom to whom custom; fear to whom fear; honor to whom honor."

Psalms 29:2

"Give unto the Lord the glory *due* unto His name; worship the Lord in the beauty of holiness."

Psalms 96:8

"Give unto the Lord the glory *due* unto his name: bring an offering, and come into His courts."

Deuteronomy 11:14

That I will give you the rain of your land in His *due* season, the first rain and the latter rain, that thou mayest gather in thy corn, and thy wine, and thine oil.

Luke 23:41

"And we indeed justly; for we receive the *due* reward of our deeds: but this man hath done nothing amiss."

1 Corinthians 7:3

> "Let the husband render unto the wife *due* benevolence: and likewise, also the wife unto the husband."

Leviticus 26:4

> "Then I will give you rain in *due season*, and the land shall yield her increase, and the trees of the field shall yield their fruit."

1 Chronicles 15:13

> "For because ye did it not at the first, the Lord our God made a breach upon us, for that we sought Him not after the *due order*.

Proverbs 15:23

> "A man hath joy by the answer of his mouth: and a word spoken in *due season*, how good is it!"

DEW

DEW

This is also the year of the DEW.

"When does the dew come?" the Lord asked. "The dew comes at night before the day," He explained. 'Weeping may endure for a night, but joy comes in the morning,' He reminded. "I will bring this dew to you as a sign and a wonder. Even as the Israelites complained in the past, so have many of you, I still provided for all of you in the wilderness. I continue to make manna from dew. You will taste and see heavenly blessings in this year. Things that cannot be explained but I will hasten My Word to perform it. For yes, the DUE Time and the DEW Time are here.

This will be a year of dew. There will be tangible moisture that will be made manifest. The dew was a sign. I am going to demonstrate through the weather and other supernatural occurrences.

According to the Merriam-Webster dictionary, *dew* is defined as water in the form of droplets that appears on thin, exposed objects in the morning or evening due to condensation.

"Dew, known in Hebrew as לט (*tal*), is significant in the Jewish religion for agricultural and theological purposes. On the first day of Passover, the *Chazan*, dressed in a white *kittel*, leads a service in which he prays for *dew* between that point and Sukkot. During the rainy season between December and Passover there are also additions in the Amidah for blessed *dew* to come together with rain. There are many midrashim that refer to *dew* as being the tool for ultimate resurrection" (Jewish Encyclopedia).

Through reading the scriptures of the Bible, there are multiple benefits of *dew*. With the *dew*, comes many things:

- Promise, inheritance
- Provision, abundance
- Distillation
- Precious things from heaven
- A sign
- Confirmation
- Joy
- Sudden source of blessing
- Peace, prosperity, fruit, increase, inheritance

Promise, the inheritance to Jacob instead of Esau.

Genesis 27:28

"Therefore, God give thee of the *dew* of heaven and the fatness of the earth and plenty of corn and wine."

Genesis 27:39

> "And Isaac his other answered and said unto him, Behold, thy dwelling shall be the fatness of the earth, and of the *dew* of heaven from above"

In Genesis 27, Isaac, the father of Jacob and Esau was approaching the end of his life. He called out to Esau, the oldest to go out to the fields, catch venison, and make him a savory dish. While Esau was out, Jacob tricked their father into giving him (Jacob)the blessing. The "*dew* of heaven and fatness of the earth and plenty of corn and wine" are the promise and inheritance.

There is no lack – but supernatural provision, miracles with dew.

Genesis 16:12-15

> [12] "I have heard the mumblings of the Israelites; speak to them, saying 'At twilight, you shall eat meat, and in the morning, you shall be filled with bread; and you shall know that I am your God.
>
> [13] So in the evening the quails came up and covered the camp, and in the morning, there was a blanket of *dew* around the camp.
>
> [14] When the layer of *dew* evaporated, on the surface of the wilderness there was a fine, flake-

like thing as fine as frost on the ground…this
is the bread of Heaven."

Numbers 11:9

"When the *dew* fell on the camp at night, the
manna fell with it."

From here, you can see that provision is being made – even
in a difficult place. The Lord said to me and I articulated,
when I ministered this in January, that even in famine, we
don't have to worry about eating. I thought it was sort of
comical when it came out of my mouth that you will eat that
hamburger you want to eat if that is your desire. You will eat.
We hadn't heard any talk of famine except for when you hear
people collecting money for foreign impoverished nations or
in the story of Joseph – not in America. The Lord used the
dew as a sign and a wonder. Even the transformation of
the *dew* from liquid into flakes, which became the bread of
Heaven for the people is supernatural. This bread/manna
is a foreshadowing of Jesus coming down from heaven to
become the manifestation and deliverance for people. The
manna was only good for that day. Daily the Lord provided
this manna for the Israelites. We, too, will see daily provision
by consuming the Word of God which is Jesus Christ.

Dew distills.

Deuteronomy 32:2

"Let my teaching drop as the rain, my speech
distill as the *dew*, As the light rain upon the

tender grass, And as the spring showers upon the herb."

Cambridge dictionary defines distillation a couple of ways:

1. The process of making a liquid stronger or purer by heating it until it changes to a gas and then cooling it so that it changes back into a liquid or a liquid made by this process:

   •Usually, the liquid is extracted by distillation.

   •The oil is a mixture of hydrocarbons that can be separated into various distillations.

2. Cambridge also defines distillation as Something that gives only the main meaning or the most important parts of something, or the action of reducing something to its main meaning or most important parts.

Encyclopedia Britannica mentions the liquid-vapor conversions of distillation. It also explains the distillation (purification process) of air, water, and crude oil required so that each substance is more fitting for various purposes.

Many of us are going through a distilling process. If any of us feel as if we are being heated up due to our present circumstances, know that God is not surprised by this. This process is purifying us, refining us, and pulling out the best of us. The distilling process brings us to a point of such heat that the impure part is separated and then purged.

In this hour, the Lord wants us to embrace the process. When the pressure and all the challenges and uncertainties are happening around us and in us, we need to be steadfast in the process. Through this, we are getting better, more essential, stronger, more precious, and able to be used in many more ways.

A way to think about this is with essential oils. The fragrance is stronger and more authentic. Allow God to purify us. Do not stop midway in the process. The end of this process is that we will be better than we were before.

This distilling is a clean-up of our heart condition. The distilling cleans our hearts and mouths when we yield to the Holy Spirit. We need sanctification (holiness) and the reverential fear of God in this hour. Yield to the process!

Dew is precious.

Deuteronomy 33:13-16

> ¹³ "And of Joseph he said, "Blessed by the Lord be his land, With the precious things of heaven, with the *dew*, and from the deep *water* that lies beneath,

> ¹⁴ With the precious fruits of the sun, and with the precious produce of the months.

> ¹⁵ With the best things of the ancient mountains, and with the precious things of the everlasting hills,

^{16} With the precious things of the earth and its
fullness, and the favor *and* goodwill of Him
who dwelt in the bush."

Because of Reuben's sin with Bilhah, Joseph received the
double blessing of the firstborn. The descendants of Joseph
became the tribes established by his two sons, Ephraim,
and Manasseh (see v. 17). As we see in Deuteronomy, *dew*
is associated with precious things. *Dew* is associated with
heaven. *Dew* is a precious blessing.

Dew shows safety.

Deuteronomy 33:28

"Israel then shall dwell in safety alone: the fountain of Jacob shall be upon a land of corn
and wine; also, His heavens shall drop down
dew."

Dew is associated with safety and provision. The falling of
the *dew* also reflects heaven's blessings.

Dew as a sign

Judges 6:36-40

Sign of the Fleece

^{36} "Then Gideon said to God, "If You are going to
rescue Israel through me, as You have spo-
ken,

³⁷ behold, I will put a fleece of [freshly sheared] wool on the threshing floor. If there is *dew* only on the fleece, and it is dry on all the ground [around it], then I will know that You will rescue Israel through me, as You have said."

³⁸ And it was so. When he got up early the next morning and squeezed the *dew* out of the fleece, he wrung from it a bowl full of water.

³⁹ Then Gideon said to God, "Do not let your anger burn against me, so that I may speak once more. Please let me make a test once more with the fleece; now let only the fleece be dry, and let there be *dew* on all the ground."

⁴⁰ God did so that night; for it was dry only on the fleece, and there was *dew* on all the ground [around it]."

In the Bible, *dew* was used as a sign as described above. God showed out through His supernatural manifestation of wetting the fleece and drying the fleece. Whether it will manifest exactly like this in modern times is unknown. But what is known is that if God did it one time, He can do it again or reverse a situation. He is God all by himself. God can use any supernatural sign He wants. That's the point here with the story of Gideon and the sign of the fleece. God prefers us to trust Him without a sign such as the fleece, but should we need a sign, He can demonstrate in multiple ways. Jesus said in John 20:29-31 that He would prefer that we believe.

We should walk by faith in His Word to us. Here's the Word straight from Jesus:

John 20:29-31

29 "Jesus responded, "Thomas, now that you've seen Me, you believe. But there are those who have never seen Me with their eyes but have believed in Me with their hearts, and they will be blessed even more!"

30 Jesus went on to do many more miraculous signs in the presence of his disciples, which are not even included in this book.

31 But all that is recorded here is so that you will fully believe that Jesus is the Anointed One, the Son of God, and that through your faith in Him you will experience eternal life by the power of His name!"

The blessing of dew.

2 Samuel 1:21

David's Dirge for Saul and Jonathan

17 "Then David sang this dirge (funeral song) over Saul and his son Jonathan,

18 and he told them to teach the sons of Judah, the song of the bow. Behold, it is written in the Book of Jashar:

¹⁹ 'Your glory and splendor, O Israel, is slain upon your high places! How the mighty have fallen!

²⁰ Tell it not in Gath; proclaim it not in the streets of Ashkelon, or the daughters of the Philistines will rejoice; the daughters of the uncircumcised (pagans) will exult.

²¹ As an expression of his grief, David curses the place of Saul's death. O mountains of Gilboa, let not *dew* or rain be upon you, nor fields with offerings, for there the shield of the mighty was defiled; the shield of Saul, [dry, cracked] not anointed with oil.

²² From the blood of the slain, from the fat of the mighty, the bow of Jonathan did not turn back, and the sword of Saul did not return empty."

In this example, we see David express his grief by cursing the place of Saul's death. Here he says, "Let not *dew* or rain be upon you..." Therefore, one would reason that if cursing is the withdrawal of *dew,* rain, or fields with offerings, then the opposite is true. The blessing is when *dew*, rain, and fields of offering are present.

Dew as unseen and unheard.

2 Samuel 17:11-14

¹¹ "But I advise that all [the men of] Israel be summoned to you, from Dan [in the north] to

Beersheba [in the south], like the sand that is by the sea in abundance, and that you personally go into battle.

¹² So shall we come upon David in one of the places where he can be found, and we will fall on him as the *dew* falls [unseen and unheard] on the ground; and of him and of all the men who are with him, not even one will be left.

¹³ If he retreats into a city, then all Israel shall bring ropes to that city, and we will drag it into the ravine until not even a pebble [of it] is found there.

¹⁴ Then Absalom and all the men of Israel said, "The advice of Hushai the Archite is better than that of Ahithophel." For the Lord had ordained to thwart the good advice of Ahithophel, so that the Lord could bring disaster upon Absalom."

The *dew* is sometimes so quiet and not seen that it can come upon us, and we do not realize it. We must be sensitive in this hour and the coming days to recognize the *dew* by sight and sound.

Dew as plenitude.

1 Kings 17:1-4

"Elijah Predicts Drought"

> [1] "Now Elijah the Tishbite, who was of the set-tlers of Gilead, said to Ahab, 'As the Lord, the God of Israel lives, before whom I stand, there shall be neither *dew* nor rain these years, except by my word.'
>
> [2] And the Word of the Lord came to him, saying,
>
> [3] 'Go from here and turn eastward and hide your-self by the brook Cherith, which is east of the Jordan [River].
>
> [4] You shall drink from the brook, and I have com-manded the ravens to sustain you there [with food].'"

In this passage, Elijah predicted the drought. According to the Merriam Webster dictionary, drought is:

1. a period of dryness especially when pro-longed, specifically one that causes exten-sive damage to crops or prevents their suc-cessful growth.

2. a prolonged or chronic shortage or lack of something expected or desired.

Therefore, one would reason that the opposite is pleni-tude. Plenitude means 1) the quality or state of being full:

COMPLETENESS or 2) a great sufficiency: ABUNDANCE. *(Merriam Webster)*

Since the Lord said in the Word of the Lord given to me, that this was our *Dew* Time, we will not see a total drought. I am firmly convinced by His word that we will begin to see abundance beginning in this year.

Dew associated with joy.

Psalms 65:12

> ¹² "The pastures of the wilderness drip [with *dew*], and the hills are encircled with joy.

> ¹³ The meadows are clothed with flocks, and the valleys are covered with grain; they shout for joy, and they sing."

Dew can be associated with joy. Who doesn't feel great when there is abundance? Remember when you received your very first paycheck? You were bouncing in your heart and filled with glee. I can see some of you singing and dancing when you got that money. In this season, what was your wilderness is going to make way for you to drip with *dew*. Get ready for this *Dew* Time. For it is coming with joy and many blessings. You can shout now! Hallelujah! Praise the Lord!

Dew associated with youth.
Psalm 110:3

> "Thou hast the *dew* of thy youth."

In this *due* season, God will give us the *dew* of our youth. Many of us will begin to look younger and fresher.

Dew in a harvest.

Isaiah 18:4 (AMP)

> "For this is what the Lord has said to me, 'I will be quiet and I will look on from My dwelling place, like shimmering heat above the sunshine, like a cloud of *dew* in the heat of harvest.'"

The harvest comes when seeds have been sown, and there has been time to germinate and become plants. Harvest is when it is time to pick that which you have sown seeds for. It is work to gather in this season, but God is going to provide a covering for us. He will give us His covering so that we can see His tangible presence amid our harvest season. He is watching over us, even when He is quiet. That's good news!

Dew is refreshing, life-giving, supernatural.

Isaiah 26:19

> "Your people will rise to life! Tell them to leave their graves and celebrate with shouts.

You refresh the earth like morning *dew*; you give life to the dead."

The *dew* is associated with a refreshing, resetting, and resuscitation by God for His people. He will bring new life to those who are alive yet feel dead. It is time to celebrate with shouts. Take off the grave clothes and come alive! God's people, arise to life! Hallelujah!

Dew, a source of blessing and replenishment, comes suddenly.

Micah 5:7 (KJV)

> "A few of Jacob's descendants survived and are scattered among the nations. But the Lord will let them cover the earth like *dew* and rain that refreshes the soil."

Micah 5:7 (AMP)

> "Then the remnant of Jacob shall be among many peoples like *dew* from the Lord, like showers on the grass [a source of blessing], which [come suddenly and] do not wait for man nor delay for the sons of men."

Even in Micah 5:7, we see God take the remnant of Jacob's descendants and begin to flourish the earth like *dew*. That's the blessings that are not dependent on man!

Sin and disobedience withhold the dew.

Haggai 1:7-10 (AMP)

> [7] "Thus says the Lord of hosts, 'Consider your ways and thoughtfully reflect on your conduct!

> [8] Go up to the hill country; bring lumber and rebuild My house (temple), that I may be pleased with it and be glorified,' says the Lord [accepting it as done for My glory].

> [9] 'You look for much [harvest], but it comes to little; and even when you bring that home, I blow it away. Why?' says the Lord of hosts. 'Because of My house, which lies in ruins while each of you runs to his own house [eager to enjoy it].

> [10] Therefore, because of you [that is, your sin and disobedience] the heavens withhold the *dew,* and the earth withholds its produce.

> [11] I called for a drought on the land and the hill country, on the grain, on the new wine, on the oil, on what the ground produces, on men, on cattle, and on all the labor of your hands.'"

Sin and disobedience will cause heaven to withhold the *dew*. With that, there is a downward spiral of earth withholding its produce, and then a ripple effect is that there is a drought on everything. If ever there was a season to obey the Lord and seek to do His way, it is now! The Lord wants us to rebuild His church and ourselves (our temples) so that He can be glorified. God is giving us an opportunity to get His house and our houses in order. We do not want the heavens to withhold the *dew*.

Peace, prosperity, fruit, increase, and inheritance of dew.

Zechariah 8:11-13 (AMP)

> [11] "'But now [in this time since you began to build] I will not treat the remnant of this people as in the former days,' declares the Lord of hosts.

> [12] 'For there the seed will produce peace and prosperity; the vine will yield its fruit, and the ground will produce its increase, and the heavens will give their *dew*. And I will cause the remnant of this people to inherit and possess all these things.

> [13] And as you have been a curse among the nations, O house of Judah (Southern Kingdom) and house of Israel (Northern Kingdom), so I will save you, that you may be a blessing. Fear not; let your hands be strong.'"

Peace, prosperity, fruitful vines, increase in the ground, and the drop down of *dew* from heaven will happen for God's remnant. We are God's remnant! To the remnant, God is saving us and blessing us. We will still have to be fearless and strong but know that since we are building His temple, we will inherit benefits.

As I was researching the word "*dew*" in the Bible, an interesting thing struck me. The last mention of "*dew*" in the Bible is in Zechariah of the Old Testament. It's the second book before the New Testament. There is no mention of *dew* in the New Testament. The Lord impressed on my heart that it is because we are that remnant. Glory!!!

DEW Scriptures for Meditation

Genesis 27:28

"Therefore, God give thee of the *dew* of heaven and the fatness of the earth and plenty of corn and wine."

Genesis 27:39

"And Isaac his other answered and said unto him, Behold, thy dwelling shall be the fatness of the earth, and of the *dew* of heaven from above..."

Genesis 16:12-15

12 "I have heard the mumblings of the Israelites; speak to them, saying 'At twilight, you shall eat meat, and in the morning, you shall be filled with bread; and you shall know that I am your God.

13 So in the evening the quails came up and covered the camp, and in the morning, there was a blanket of *dew* around the camp.

14 When the layer of *dew* evaporated, on the surface of the wilderness there was a fine, flake-like thing as fine as frost on the ground.... this is the bread of Heaven."

Numbers 11:9

"When the *dew* fell on the camp at night, the manna fell with it."

Deuteronomy 32:2

"Let my teaching drop as the rain, my speech distill as the *dew*, As the light rain upon the tender grass, and as the spring showers upon the herb."

Deuteronomy 33:28 (AMP)

"Israel then shall dwell in safety alone; the fountain of Jacob shall be upon a land of corn and wine; also, His heavens shall drop down *dew*."

DO

DO

The Lord said, *"This is the time to DO. It is time to just do it. There are things that you have put on the back burner. There will be time to do hobbies and things that you said that you never had time to do. Do it. I am calling you to do what I called you to do. Even as Deuteronomy talks about the dos. I'm calling you to be a 'do-it-er on me.' The book gives you to do and not to do. I tell you what not to do. This is not a time to do what is wrong or rather disobey. Obedience is better than sacrifice. Do what I called you to do. In Deuteronomy 28, I tell you what to do and not to do. Also, remember My Word in Deuteronomy 8:18 where I give you the power to get wealth."*

DO

This is the time to do. According to the Book of Nike (lol), "Just *do* it". The Lord said there are so many things that you want to *do*. He said that He is giving us the time to *do* it. Little did I know at the beginning of the year when the Lord gave that word, how this would come to pass. In March and April of 2020, we witnessed the world come to a pause with COVID-19, the coronavirus pandemic. Except for doctors, nurses, and other front-line personnel, most have been quarantined to their houses. It pushed many to *do* the household tasks and other projects pushed aside for months and years. Some have taken extra-curricular courses and webinars to expand their knowledge base in given or several areas. Others have taken up hobbies such as learning to play the guitar, piano, or other instruments or improved their cooking skills. God did say there would be time to *do* hobbies. We have had to learn to be creative with our time and resources. The power of having the internet to communicate and learn has been a blessing. Many families who never had time to be together have had more time within these two months than in the past to *do* family things together.

While God did not create this pandemic, He is allowing His people the opportunity to be reset for His glory and also for their pleasure. Romans 8:28 says, "And we know that all things work together for good to those who love God, to those who are the called according to His purpose." Notice He calls us "the called." He is not just calling us; we are already purposed. In Jeremiah 29:11-13 God reassures us:

> For I know the thoughts that I think toward you,
> says the Lord, thoughts of peace and not of
> evil, to give you a future and a hope. Then
> you will call upon Me and go and pray to Me,
> and I will listen to you. And you will seek Me
> and find Me, when you search for Me with all
> your heart.

In this season, many who had drifted away from the Lord, found themselves recommitting to Him. This is a time to seek God while He may be found. More have started to pray. With so much unknown about the coronavirus, it has caused many to drop to their knees and pray. With this many will find themselves out of their comfort zones. I am one. During this time, the Lord called me to *do* what I did not necessarily want to *do*. He had me to go on Facebook Live every day at 9:30 pm to read the Psalm that corresponded with the day and read Psalms 91 for 30 consecutive days. He then instructed me to *do* 10 additional days of praying on-line. For a total of 40 days, people from Houston, other parts of the United States, and all over the world would join me to read along with the Psalms. In the midst of this, I had to learn how to shuffle things around and make God the priority. This was my test. We must always make room for Him.

What is God calling you to *do* in terms of your relationship with Him? Are you reading His Word? Are you fasting, tithing, or just being still? When was the last time you just asked Him what He desired? Simply ask Him, "What do you want me to *do*, Lord? How can I please you, Lord?" Have you called out to Him this season?

During this time, the Lord will show up in the most unusual ways. He wants so much to commune with us. While the quarantined lifestyle has allowed us time to work on our "back burner projects and desires," it is not a time to sacrifice a committed and holy lifestyle.

When I ministered this word in early January, the Lord specifically spoke about this not being the time to do certain things. This is not the time to miss the mark with sanctification and holiness. Simply put, this was a time for unmarried people to keep their zippers up and legs closed. I was surprised to hear these words even come out of my mouth, but the fire of the Lord was upon me.

The Lord shared that there is so much He wants to *do* for us. I do not believe that has changed. We are on the brink of the greatest turnarounds that the world has seen. This is a *Shakeup*, for the *Wake up* for us to *Go up*! The Lord desires to promote us to the next level, but there was and is some alignment that is needed. He could have us go up with a shaky foundation. However, He is solidifying us. He was fixing our foundation for the new levels to be placed on top.

"Get ready," I heard the Lord say. "Many have had more rest than you have had in months and Sundays. Yes, there will be restoration, but there will also be more that is required for you to *do*." Isaiah 60:2 says, "For, behold, the darkness shall cover the earth, and gross darkness the people: but the Lord shall arise upon thee, and His glory shall be seen upon thee." We are called to be the light in this earth.

Not everyone will decide to keep the trajectory of pursuing the Lord. Many will go back to old ways and habits. For some who did not secure themselves in this season, their minds will go to a reprobate mindset. We must continue to pray especially that our loved ones and family stay under the wings of the Lord. No fear. God has not given us a spirit of fear but of power, love, and a sound mind (2 Timothy 1:7). He wants to *do* the very best for His own. So, continue to *do* what He has asked and called you to *do*.

Scriptures with Do

Deuteronomy 28:1-68

[1] "And it shall come to pass, if thou shalt hearken diligently unto the voice of the Lord thy God, to observe and to *do* all his commandments which I command thee this day, that the Lord thy God will set thee on high above all nations of the earth:

[2] And all these blessings shall come on thee, and overtake thee, if thou shalt hearken unto the voice of the Lord thy God.

[3] Blessed shalt thou be in the city, and blessed shalt thou be in the field.

[4] Blessed shall be the fruit of thy body, and the fruit of thy ground, and the fruit of thy cattle, the increase of thy kine, and the flocks of thy sheep.

[5] Blessed shall be thy basket and thy store.

[6] Blessed shalt thou be when thou comest in, and blessed shalt thou be when thou goest out.

⁷ The Lord shall cause thine enemies that rise up against thee to be smitten before thy face: they shall come out against thee one way, and flee before thee seven ways.

⁸ The Lord shall command the blessing upon thee in thy storehouses, and in all that thou settest thine hand unto; and He shall bless thee in the land which the Lord thy God giveth thee.

⁹ The Lord shall establish thee an holy people unto Himself, as He hath sworn unto thee, if thou shalt keep the commandments of the Lord thy God, and walk in His ways.

¹⁰ And all people of the earth shall see that thou art called by the name of the Lord; and they shall be afraid of thee.

¹¹ And the Lord shall make thee plenteous in goods, in the fruit of thy body, and in the fruit of thy cattle, and in the fruit of thy ground, in the land which the Lord sware unto thy fathers to give thee.

¹² The Lord shall open unto thee his good treasure, the heaven to give the rain unto thy land in his season, and to bless all the work of thine hand: and thou shalt lend unto many nations, and thou shalt not borrow.

¹³ And the Lord shall make thee the head, and not the tail; and thou shalt be above only, and thou shalt not be beneath; if that thou hearken unto the commandments of the Lord thy God, which I command thee this day, to observe and to do them:

¹⁴ And thou shalt not go aside from any of the words which I command thee this day, to the right hand, or to the left, to go after other gods to serve them.

¹⁵ But it shall come to pass, if thou wilt not hearken unto the voice of the Lord thy God, to observe to *do* all His commandments and His statutes which I command thee this day; that all these curses shall come upon thee, and overtake thee:

¹⁶ Cursed shalt thou be in the city, and cursed shalt thou be in the field.

¹⁷ Cursed shall be thy basket and thy store.

¹⁸ Cursed shall be the fruit of thy body, and the fruit of thy land, the increase of thy kine, and the flocks of thy sheep.

¹⁹ Cursed shalt thou be when thou comest in, and cursed shalt thou be when thou goest out.

²⁰ The Lord shall send upon thee cursing, vexation, and rebuke, in all that thou settest thine

hand unto for to do, until thou be destroyed, and until thou perish quickly; because of the wickedness of thy doings, whereby thou hast forsaken me.

21 The Lord shall make the pestilence cleave unto thee, until He has consumed thee from off the land, whither thou goest to possess it.

22 The Lord shall smite thee with a consumption, and with a fever, and with an inflammation, and with an extreme burning, and with the sword, and with blasting, and with mildew; and they shall pursue thee until thou perish.

23 And thy heaven that is over thy head shall be brass, and the earth that is under thee shall be iron.

24 The Lord shall make the rain of thy land powder and dust: from heaven shall it come down upon thee, until thou be destroyed.

25 The Lord shall cause thee to be smitten before thine enemies: thou shalt go out one way against them, and flee seven ways before them: and shalt be removed into all the kingdoms of the earth.

26 And thy carcass shall be meat unto all fowls of the air, and unto the beasts of the earth, and no man shall fray them away.

²⁷ The Lord will smite thee with the botch of Egypt, and with the emerods, and with the scab, and with the itch, whereof thou canst not be healed.

²⁸ The Lord shall smite thee with madness, and blindness, and astonishment of heart:

²⁹ And thou shalt grope at noonday, as the blind gropeth in darkness, and thou shalt not prosper in thy ways: and thou shalt be only oppressed and spoiled evermore, and no man shall save thee.

³⁰ Thou shalt betroth a wife, and another man shall lie with her: thou shalt build a house, and thou shalt not dwell therein: thou shalt plant a vineyard, and shalt not gather the grapes thereof.

³¹ Thine ox shall be slain before thine eyes, and thou shalt not eat thereof: thine ass shall be violently taken away from before thy face, and shall not be restored to thee: thy sheep shall be given unto thine enemies, and thou shalt have none to rescue them.

³² Thy sons and thy daughters shall be given unto another people, and thine eyes shall look, and fail with longing for them all the day long: and there shall be no might in thine hand.

³³ The fruit of thy land, and all thy labours, shall a nation which thou knowest not eat up; and thou shalt be only oppressed and crushed alway:

³⁴ So that thou shalt be mad for the sight of thine eyes which thou shalt see.

³⁵ The Lord shall smite thee in the knees, and in the legs, with a sore botch that cannot be healed, from the sole of thy foot unto the top of thy head.

³⁶ The Lord shall bring thee, and thy king which thou shalt set over thee, unto a nation which neither thou nor thy fathers have known; and there shalt thou serve other gods, wood and stone.

³⁷ And thou shalt become an astonishment, a proverb, and a byword, among all nations whither the Lord shall lead thee.

³⁸ Thou shalt carry much seed out into the field, and shalt gather but little in; for the locust shall consume it.

³⁹ Thou shalt plant vineyards, and dress them, but shalt neither drink of the wine, nor gather the grapes; for the worms shall eat them.

⁴⁰ Thou shalt have olive trees throughout all thy coasts, but thou shalt not anoint thyself with the oil; for thine olive shall cast his fruit.

[41] Thou shalt beget sons and daughters, but thou shalt not enjoy them; for they shall go into captivity.

[42] All thy trees and fruit of thy land shall the locust consume.

[43] The stranger that is within thee shall get up above thee very high; and thou shalt come down very low.

[44] He shall lend to thee, and thou shalt not lend to him: he shall be the head, and thou shalt be the tail.

[45] Moreover all these curses shall come upon thee, and shall pursue thee, and overtake thee, till thou be destroyed; because thou hearkenedst not unto the voice of the Lord thy God, to keep His commandments and His statutes which He commanded thee:

[46] And they shall be upon thee for a sign and for a wonder, and upon thy seed forever.

[47] Because thou servedst not the Lord thy God with joyfulness, and with gladness of heart, for the abundance of all things;

[48] Therefore shalt thou serve thine enemies which the Lord shall send against thee, in hunger, and in thirst, and in nakedness, and in want of all things: and He shall put a yoke of iron upon thy neck, until He have destroyed thee.

[49] The Lord shall bring a nation against thee from far, from the end of the earth, as swift as the eagle flieth; a nation whose tongue thou shalt not understand;

[50] A nation of fierce countenance, which shall not regard the person of the old, nor shew favour to the young:

[51] And he shall eat the fruit of thy cattle, and the fruit of thy land, until thou be destroyed: which also shall not leave thee either corn, wine, or oil, or the increase of thy kine, or flocks of thy sheep, until he have destroyed thee.

[52] And he shall besiege thee in all thy gates, until thy high and fenced walls come down, wherein thou trustedst, throughout all thy land: and he shall besiege thee in all thy gates throughout all thy land, which the Lord thy God hath given thee.

[53] And thou shalt eat the fruit of thine own body, the flesh of thy sons and of thy daughters, which the Lord thy God hath given thee, in the siege, and in the straitness, wherewith thine enemies shall distress thee:

[54] So that the man that is tender among you, and very delicate, his eye shall be evil toward his brother, and toward the wife of his bosom,

and toward the remnant of his children which he shall leave:

⁵⁵ So that he will not give to any of them of the flesh of his children whom he shall eat: because he hath nothing left him in the siege, and in the straitness, wherewith thine enemies shall distress thee in all thy gates.

⁵⁶ The tender and delicate woman among you, which would not adventure to set the sole of her foot upon the ground for delicateness and tenderness, her eye shall be evil toward the husband of her bosom, and toward her son, and toward her daughter,

⁵⁷And toward her young one that cometh out from between her feet, and toward her children which she shall bear: for she shall eat them for want of all things secretly in the siege and straitness, wherewith thine enemy shall distress thee in thy gates.

⁵⁸ If thou wilt not observe to do all the words of this law that are written in this book, that thou mayest fear this glorious and fearful name, THE LORD THY GOD;

⁵⁹ Then the Lord will make thy plagues wonderful, and the plagues of thy seed, even great plagues, and of long continuance, and sore sicknesses, and of long continuance.

⁶⁰ Moreover He will bring upon thee all the diseases of Egypt, which thou wast afraid of; and they shall cleave unto thee.

⁶¹ Also every sickness, and every plague, which is not written in the book of this law, them will the Lord bring upon thee, until thou be destroyed.

⁶² And ye shall be left few in number, whereas ye were as the stars of heaven for multitude; because thou wouldest not obey the voice of the Lord thy God.

⁶³ And it shall come to pass, that as the Lord rejoiced over you to do you good, and to multiply you; so the Lord will rejoice over you to destroy you, and to bring you to nought; and ye shall be plucked from off the land whither thou goest to possess it.

⁶⁴ And the Lord shall scatter thee among all people, from the one end of the earth even unto the other; and there thou shalt serve other gods, which neither thou nor thy fathers have known, even wood and stone.

⁶⁵ And among these nations shalt thou find no ease, neither shall the sole of thy foot have rest: but the Lord shall give thee there a trembling heart, and failing of eyes, and sorrow of mind:

⁶⁶ And thy life shall hang in doubt before thee; and thou shalt fear day and night, and shalt have none assurance of thy life:

⁶⁷ In the morning thou shalt say, 'Would God it were even!' And at even thou shalt say, 'Would God it were morning!' for the fear of thine heart wherewith thou shalt fear, and for the sight of thine eyes which thou shalt see.

⁶⁸ And the Lord shall bring thee into Egypt again with ships, by the way whereof I spake unto thee, Thou shalt see it no more again: and there ye shall be sold unto your enemies for bondmen and bondwomen, and no man shall buy you."

Zechariah 8:14-23 (AMP)

¹⁴ "For thus says the Lord of hosts, 'Just as I planned to *do* harm to you when your fathers provoked Me to wrath,' says the Lord of hosts, 'and I did not relent,

¹⁵ so I have again planned in these days to *do* good to Jerusalem and to the house of Judah. *Do* not fear!

¹⁶ These are the things which you should *do*: speak the truth with one another; judge with truth and pronounce the judgment that brings peace in [the courts at] your gates.

¹⁷ And let none of you devise or even imagine evil in your heart against another, and *do* not love lying or half-truths; for all these things I hate,' declares the Lord.

¹⁸ Then the word of the Lord of hosts came to me (Zechariah), saying,

¹⁹ Thus says the Lord of hosts, 'The fast of the fourth [month to mourn the breaching of Jerusalem's walls], the fast of the fifth [month to mourn the temple's destruction], the fast of the seventh [month to mourn Gedaliah's assassination], and the fast of the tenth [month to mourn the siege of Jerusalem] will become times of joy and gladness and cheerful feasts for the house of Judah; so [to bring this about] love truth and peace.'

²⁰ Thus says the Lord of hosts, 'It will come to pass that peoples and the inhabitants of many cities will come [to Jerusalem].

²¹ The inhabitants of one [city] will go to another, saying, 'Let us go at once to ask the favor of the Lord and to seek the Lord of hosts. I will go also.

²² So many peoples and powerful nations will come to seek the Lord of hosts in Jerusalem and to ask the Lord for His favor.'

[23] Thus says the Lord of hosts, 'In those days ten men [as representatives] from all the nations will grasp the robe of a Jew, saying, 'Let us go with you, for we have heard that God is with you.'"

Colossians 3:23 (KJV)

"And whatsoever ye *do*, *do* it heartily, as to the Lord, and not unto men;"

Colossians 3:17 (KJV)

"And whatsoever ye *do* in word or deed, *do* all in the name of the Lord Jesus, giving thanks to God and the Father by Him."

Philippians 4:13 (KJV)

"I can *do* all things through Christ which strengtheneth me."

Philippians 2:13 (KJV)

"For it is God which worketh in you both to will and to *do* of his good pleasure."

Colossians 3:13 (KJV)

"Forbearing one another, and forgiving one another, if any man has a quarrel against any: even as Christ forgave you, so also *do* ye."

Ephesians 3:20 (KJV)

"Now unto Him that is able to *do* exceeding abundantly above all that we ask or think, according to the power that worketh in us,"

Philippians 4:9 (KJV)

"Those things, which ye have both learned, and received, and heard, and seen in me, *do*: and the God of peace shall be with you."

Mark 10:19 (KJV)

"Thou knowest the commandments: *Do* not commit adultery; *Do* not kill; *Do* not steal; *Do* not bear false witness; defraud not; honour thy father and mother."

Luke 18:20 (KJV)

"Thou knowest the commandments: *Do* not commit adultery; *Do* not kill; *Do* not steal; *Do* not bear false witness; Honour thy father and thy mother."

Psalms 58:1 (KJV)

"*Do* ye indeed speak righteousness, O congregation? *do* ye judge uprightly, O ye sons of men?"

Luke 6:31 (KJV)

"And as ye would that men should *do* to you, *do* ye also to them likewise."

1 Corinthians 12:30 (KJV)

"Have all the gifts of healing? *Do all* speak with tongues? *Do* all interpret?"

Daniel 11:32 (KJV)

"And such as do wickedly against the covenant shall he corrupt by flatteries: but the people that *do* know their God shall be strong, and *do* exploits."

Matthew 23:3 (KJV)

"All therefore whatsoever they bid you observe, that observe and *do*; but do not ye after their works: for they say, and *do not*."

Luke 6:33 (KJV)

"And if ye *do* good to them which *do* good to you, what thank have ye? For sinners also *do* even the same."

Philippians 3:13 (KJV)

"Brethren, I count not myself to have apprehend-ed: but this one thing I *do*, forgetting those things which are behind, and reaching forth unto those things which are before,"

John 15:5 (KJV)

"I am the vine, ye are the branches: He that abideth in me, and I in him, the same bringeth forth much fruit: for without me ye can *do* nothing."

Matthew 5:44 (KJV)

"But I say unto you, 'Love your enemies, bless them that curse you, *do* good to them that hate you, and pray for them which despitefully use you, and persecute you;'"

Numbers 33:56 (KJV)

"Moreover, it shall come to pass, that I shall *do* unto you, as I thought to *do* unto them."

Deuteronomy 25:16 (KJV)

"For all that *do* such things, and all that do unrighteously, are an abomination unto the Lord thy God."

Deuteronomy 29:9 (KJV)

"Keep therefore the words of this covenant, and *do* them, that ye may prosper in all that ye *do*."

Matthew 5:47 (KJV)

"And if ye salute your brethren only, what *do* ye more than others? do not even the publicans so?"

1 Corinthians 10:31 (KJV)

"Whether therefore ye eat, or drink, or whatsoever ye *do*, *do* all to the glory of God."

Psalms 31:23 (KJV)

"O love the Lord, all ye his saints: for the Lord preserveth the faithful, and plentifully rewardeth the proud *doer*."

James 1:22 (NLT)

"But don't just listen to God's word. You must *do* what it says. Otherwise, you are only fooling yourselves."

DEUX

DEUX

As I was studying the scriptures with dew, due, and do, the Lord said, *"There is another 'do'."* "I asked Him, "What "do"? He continued patiently speak to me with an accented "do." With emphasis, I asked again, *"do?"* He confirmed, "Yes, 'do'." *There is a French word which is a "do".* So, I looked it up and there it was *"DEUX".* Deux is the number two. *The Lord shared that this is the year 2020. "Twenty (20) is redemption and even in the fullness of time, I have come," he explained. "I will give you a double redemption. I will restore to you that which the locust, cankerworm, and palmerworm have taken from you (Joel 2:25). Two is the number of witnesses. There will be greater evangelism." Then the Lord advised, "Go forth especially in twos to do greater evangelism. Some have begun to say that 2020 is the year of vision, but it is also 5780* (Hebraic calendar) *which is of the mouth. You must speak. One can bring a thousand to flight but two can bring 10,000 to flight. It will take at least two to participate – one to speak and one to listen. Two (2) means double. Double blessings. As I spoke in James 5:7, I want you to be patient, for the early and latter rain are coming. That's two (2), the DEUX!"*

When I look back at this encounter with the Lord, I have to chuckle. I'm one who has studied several languages but not French. The Lord is always expanding the way that I look at things. As I think about this, He would take something that I know nothing about.

So, as I look more closely into *"Deux"*. Yes, the number two is witness. The Bible says that *two* are better than one (Ecclesiastes 4:9). In this season, you will see unique collaborations in the world. Companies that you never would consider folding will fold. There will also be strong entities that will come together in partnership. "I am expecting this of my people for greater collaborations that will bring Me glory," said the Lord. When *two* people or entities come together, one may consider that a covenant.

Below is a definition of "covenant" from *Baker's Evangelical Dictionary of Biblical Theology*:

> "The term 'covenant' is of Latin origin (con venire), meaning a coming together. It presupposes *two* or more parties who come together to make a contract, agreeing on promises, stipulations, privileges, and responsibilities. In religious and theological circles there has not been agreement on precisely what is to be understood by the biblical term. It is used variously in biblical contexts. In political situations, it can be translated treaty; in a social setting, it means a lifelong friendship agreement; or it can refer to a marriage."

"Can *two* walk together unless they be agreed?" (Amos 3:3)

You will see the distinction at this hour. There will be break-ing away from familiar toxic relationships. You will also see the coming together of God-breathed marriages towards the end of 2020 into 2021. Dynamic *duos*. "I'm enabling you," said the Lord. "Some have become comfortable with being single, but I have purposed that you do not walk alone. I am giving you this word to prepare...so walk with me daily and allow me to prepare you for the next leg of your journey. Strengthen our covenant. For yes, 20 represents redemp-tion, and I am bringing you into a fullness that you have not known."

Double redemption,
double blessings,
double favor,
double honor,
double portion,
double-take

Yes. You will wipe your eyes to see if it's real.... You are going to do a *'double-take'*." For the benefit of our interna-tional readers, the definition of a "d*ouble-take*" is a "delayed reaction to a surprising or significant situation with failure to notice anything unusual." You will do a *double-take*. Just as the apostles in John 21:26, they laid out their nets all night and caught nothing. When Jesus told them to cast down their nets again, it was so much. There was an abundance. I know many were watching with their mouths wide open. They had to do a *double-take*....and then move quickly to pull in the nets for the multitude. Yes, this is a great season of provision, favor, honor, and blessings. It is also a time of the great catch for souls into the kingdom of God. Be ready to pull in these "fish." Have you created the capacity to bring them into the boats (churches) and disciple them?

So much is going to happen, it's going to make your head swim. (Amos 9:13 Message Bible). As you read this, you may be in a still place and not much is happening.... Don't be dismayed for the Lord is telling you to hold on - that change is coming.

What's in your hands? God will take what's in your *two* hands and make it plenty. Remember the young boy who had *two* fish and some bread? Offer it up to God and bless it! Miracles are happening in this season. However, the first step is obedience.

This is the time of the *double-double*! Have you heard this term before? I had not. I looked it up. The double-double has two definitions:

1. Canadian- a cup of coffee with a *double* serving of both sugar and cream

2. Basketball- the achievement of a *double-digit* total of statistical categories (assists, blocks, points, rebounds, and steals) over the course of a single game.

Wow! The Lord blessed me to let me know what was black (as in coffee) will now be full of *double* sweetness and light. We will taste and see how good He is. We will experience His richness -the modern "milk and honey"!!! He's going to take that dark situation in our lives and turn it for His glory and our delight!

Did He take away the dark? No. He added so much to it that the darkness did not have the bitter taste!!!

There will still be darkness in the land, but God is looking out for His people. Please note that the rain will fall on the just and the unjust, but God is definitely looking out for His people.

As I write, I want to run around the block, but His word needs to get out. So, let's just shout "Hallelujah" right now!!!

Ok, let's go to the basketball definition. God is going to give us the grace to achieve more. We will see combinations of five-fold ministry gifts to win the game. There will be times when we assist, block, make points, rebound, and steal. The *double-double* is important because, in this hour, you can't only do one thing- making the shot/basket. Your achievement in this hour is for the *double-double*. Your *double-double* reward is when you assist others, block the devil, make rebounds by helping those who missed the mark to recover, and stealing (delivering) our families and friends out of the clutches of the enemy.

The harvest is plenty and laborers are few so strive to *double-up* for this special honor, five-fold gifts. *Double* portion anointing is upon us. Just like Elisha asked of Elijah and caught the mantle that was ripped into *two*. For his faithfulness and being at the right place at the right time, Elisha received the *double portion* anointing.

Just as in Job 42:10, "And the Lord turned the captivity of Job, when he prayed for his friends: also, the Lord gave Job *twice* as much as he had before." God is going to give us *double* for the trouble.

The Lord said, "In this hour, no man will take My glory." We are moving into the dimensions of God…. We will see that in this hour we will go past the 20 -20 which is equivalent of 40 of the hard times, of wilderness, of struggle to His newness and fullness of the cycle. For this is the *Due* Time beyond dimension; it is the fullness of time-*Due*; it is our *Dew* Time; it is our *Do* Time, and it is our *Deux* Time for this year and beyond.

From grade school, we all know that 2 +2 = 4. Four is the number of creativity and creation. So, in this 2020 season of vision and beyond, it is even more critical for us to use our mouths in this 5780 Hebraic year to create that which we want to see in our lives, cities, states, countries, and world. When God used His voice to create the heavens, the earth, man, the living things, and more, certainly, we do not think that we are exempt. Open your mouth and come in agreement with what God has promised you. For the plans that God has for you are good and not evil!

The best way of expressing this is what I heard in a song by Israel Houghton which says, "Say what you heard so you can see what you say. Pray these words: Take the limits off! Take the limits off! Take the limits off!"

Scriptures with Double

Exodus 22:1-4

1 "If a man shall steal an ox, or a sheep, and kill it, or sell it; he shall restore five oxen for an ox, and four sheep for a sheep.

2 If a thief be found breaking up, and be smitten that he die; there shall no blood be shed for him.

3 If the sun be risen upon him, there shall be blood shed for him; for he should make full restitution; if he have nothing, then he shall be sold for his theft.

4 If the theft be certainly found in his hand alive, whether it be ox, or ass, or sheep; he shall restore *double*."

Deuteronomy 21:15-17

15 "If a man has two wives, one beloved, and another hated, and they have born him chil-

dren, both the beloved and the hated; and if the firstborn son be hers that was hated:

¹⁶ Then it shall be, when he maketh his sons to inherit that which he hath, that he may not make the son of the beloved firstborn before the son of the hated, which is indeed the first-born:

¹⁷ But he shall acknowledge the son of the hat-ed for the firstborn, by giving him a *double* portion of all that he hath: for he is the begin-ning of his strength; the right of the firstborn is his."

2 Kings 2:9

"And it came to pass, when they were gone over, that Elijah said unto Elisha, 'Ask what I shall do for thee, before I be taken away from thee.' And Elisha said, 'I pray thee, let a *dou-ble* portion of thy spirit be upon me.'"

Isaiah 61:6-7

⁶ "But ye shall be named the Priests of the Lord: men shall call you the Ministers of our God: ye shall eat the riches of the Gentiles, and in their glory shall ye boast yourselves.

⁷ For your shame ye shall have *double*; and for confusion they shall rejoice in their portion:

therefore, in their land they shall possess the *double*: everlasting joy shall be unto them."

1 Timothy 5:17

[17] "Let the elders that rule well be counted worthy of *double* honour, especially they who labour in the word and doctrine.

[18] For the scripture saith, thou shalt not muzzle the ox that treadeth out the corn. And, the labourer is worthy of his reward."

Scriptures with Two

1 Corinthians 14:29

"Let the prophets speak *two* or three, and let the other judge."

Ephesians 5:31

"For this cause shall a man leave his father and mother, and shall be joined unto his wife, and they *two* shall be one flesh."

Mark 6:7

And He called unto Him the twelve, and began to send them forth by *two* and *two*; and gave them power over unclean spirits;

Mark 11:1

"And when they came nigh to Jerusalem, unto Bethphage and Bethany, at the Mount of Olives, He sendeth forth *two* of His disciples,"

Mark 14:13

"And He sendeth forth *two* of His disciples, and saith unto them, 'Go ye into the city, and there shall meet you a man bearing a pitcher of water: follow him.'"

Matthew 18:19-20

"Again, I say unto you, that if *two* of you shall agree on earth as touching anything that they shall ask, it shall be done for them of My Father which is in heaven. For where *two* or three are gathered in My name, there am I in the midst of them."

Luke 10:1

"After these things the Lord appointed other seventy also, and sent them *two* and *two* before his face into every city and place, wither he himself would come."

Revelation 11:3

"And I will give power unto my *two* witnesses, and they shall prophesy a thousand *two* hundred and threescore days, clothed in sackcloth.

Job 13:20

"Only do not *two* things unto me: then will I not hide myself from thee. Withdraw thine hand far from me: and let not thy dread make me afraid. Then call thou, and I will answer: or let me speak, and answer thou me. How many are mine iniquities and sins? Make me to know my transgression and my sin."

Proverbs 30:7

"*Two* things I have required of you; do not deny me them before I die: Remove vanity and lies far from me- give me neither poverty nor riches; feed me with food convenient for me; lest I be full, and deny You; and say, 'Who is the Lord?' Or lest I be poor, and steal, and take the name of my God in vain."

Ecclesiastes 4:9

"*Two* are better than one; because they have a good reward for their labour."

Ecclesiastes 4:11

"Again, if *two* lie together, then they have heat: but how can one be warm alone."

EPILOGUE

EPILOGUE

After the e-book was released, the Lord shared that He wanted me to write an epilogue to this book. I kept seeing the word "epilogue" when I would wake up from sleeping for several days.

I thought I had written all that He wanted to have me to say. However, the Lord impressed upon me the conclusion of the matter concerning due, dew, do, and deux. Can you say after me, "The end of a thing is better than the beginning?"

As for me in the season, I have had to endure a lot. This has been the case for many of you too. Your heart might have been broken by one thing or another – your health could have been challenged; your family relationships might have been strained; your finances have been tapped to go in another direction than your savings account...need I go on? The one thing I do know is that the Word of God is a sure thing, and I stand on His word.

When the Word from the Lord is delivered, not only do you hear it, but so do the forces of darkness. The enemy will attempt to thwart or even delay the Word to discourage you. I want to encourage you today that delay is not denial. The end of a thing is better than the beginning (Ecclesiastes 7:8). I want to let you know that God is intentional about our lives. We must be intentional about leaning and trusting in Him.

The Lord brought me to the book of Nehemiah in the Bible. I asked the Lord why the book of Nehemiah? What does it have to do with this book (The Due [Dü] Season)? The Lord had me to zero in on two words. The two words were the "twentieth year." As many times as I have read the book of Nehemiah, I never remember seeing that.

As it was the 20th year of King Artaxerxes' reign in the book of Nehemiah, it is the 20th year in 2000 AD (at the time this book was written) making it 2020. God is impressing on His people today as He was in the book of Nehemiah to rebuild His church. Let me back up to give you full context.

Nehemiah had received some bad news that Jerusalem was in a terrible place. The walls of Jerusalem were broken down; the gates were burned with fire, and the remnant of Jews were in great affliction. When Nehemiah heard this news, he sat down, wept, mourned for days, and fasted and prayed. Nehemiah was the cupbearer to King Artaxerxes. This was a high position of trust as this person was extremely close to the king and was charged with the responsibility to protect the king and nobility from poison. It was noted that the king had never seen Nehemiah with a sad countenance. However, Nehemiah was not sad but had sorrow in his heart. The king granted Nehemiah favor to take a leave of absence and rebuild the walls of Jerusalem.

Off went Nehemiah to Jerusalem where he inspected the ruins. There was so much to repair. However, he was able to get different Jewish family groups to come together to rebuild the wall by different sections. I can imagine that the task was huge with a wall strong enough and tall enough to fortify a city. Also, it must have been extensive because the only way that the Jewish people knew to stop working on the wall for the day was because of the sound of the trumpet which indicated quitting time. When two guys, Sanballat and Tobiah the Ammonite, heard that the Jewish people were rebuilding the wall, they mocked them and wanted to block their work. Actually, they wanted to destroy it. In Nehemiah 4:6-8, it states, "So built we the wall; and all the wall was joined together unto they held thereof: for the people had a mind to work. But it came to pass, that when Sanballat, and Tobiah, and the Arabians, and the Ammonites, and the Ashdodites heard that the walls of Jerusalem were made up, and the breaches began to be stopped, then they were very wroth, and conspired all of them together to come *and* to fight against Jerusalem, and to hinder it."

Nonetheless, the Jewish people prayed but also took up their tools and weapons to have at their side to build the wall and fight if necessary. Let me just interject in the story, that even you may have started a project, business, ministry, and all is going well, but now you have begun to face certain challenges, whether internal or external (what is happening around you). Please note that even in the time which looked like poverty and famine in the land, provision was made for Nehemiah and all who worked on the wall.

We are not unlike the Jewish people. Today, many are facing evictions and shortages, but when we all come together and make God's house a priority, provision is made. When you set yourself like the Jewish people did to follow God, you may have one or two challenges (Sanballat and Tobiah) which seem to grow to more challenges (all the other enemies). Don't give up! Pray! Take up your weapons, but continue to build.

This gigantic wall around Jerusalem was built in record-breaking time – 52 days! Imagine what we can do, when we put our minds together on a project. God wants us to *do* this. Let denominations who say that God is who He is to them, come together and build His church. Repair the wall. Right now, there are so many breaches in the wall (the church), that the enemy has come to take our children, land, and our freedoms. The enemy has come for you to back down off of your assignment with God. Discouragement has set in with many because it looks like it is impossible. God is calling us to be steadfast in our pursuit of Him. He is calling us to make sure that nothing stands in the way of us building our defense up and getting the job done. In this time, the Lord is calling us to *do* what is past *due*. Build Him up! Give Him the honor that He is *due*. It is *Due* Time to pray, worship, and remain fixed on the tasks that He has given us to *do*. It is time to roll up our sleeves, Church.

Some may say, I have already been doing this. That's great. Now is the time to partner to accomplish more for the

Kingdom. We must decrease that the Lord increases in us and our efforts. It is no longer I who lives but the Christ who lives within me. It is *Due* Time to take away selfish ambitions. When we yield to the Holy Spirit and sacrificial love as Jesus did, we are going to see mind-blowing results. Yes, this a portal in time which has been set aside for the *Due Season*. I encourage you to walk in it. Lay aside every weight that tries to weigh you down. Stop holding on to the old and embrace the new. New, new, new. His mercies are new every morning. Just as the *dew* that rests on the leaves, grass, and trees comes in the early morning. The Lord wants us to let go of yesterday and embrace His *dew*. Rest in the *dew* that comes in the stillness of the morning. "Don't forget me," says the Lord. "Make your way to Me and bring others. Divorce your old ways of doing things and trust in Me for new instructions and guidance. This is a time when I'm calling you to hear My voice among the negative voices of the world. Don't forget your sisters and brothers. Reach out again to those who may have turned you down. *Do* it again for me." As I type, I feel the fire of God all over me. I feel the Lord wanting us to extend the gift of salvation to our families, friends, and others. If immediate results come, fantastic! Praise God! Plant the seed in this *dew* season, while the ground has moisture, and it is wet. The Bible talks about one planting and the other one watering, but God is the one who gives the increase. Plant, plant, plant! If you are reading this and want to enter into the *due*, *dew*, *do* and *deux* season but haven't accepted the gift of salvation, we have good news! You can *do* it right now. Here's a simple prayer that

Billy Graham, one of the greatest evangelists, said to lead multitudes of people in salvation. Say it aloud and accept your salvation today. Hallelujah!

Prayer of Salvation

Dear Lord Jesus, I know that I am a sinner, and I ask for Your forgiveness. I believe You died for my sins and rose from the dead. I turn from my sins and invite You to come into my heart and life. I want to trust and follow You as my Lord and Savior. In Your Name. Amen.

Dunamis

Now there is another thing that the Lord wants me to leave everyone with in this Dü Season. He wants to make sure that you have yet another dü! The Lord wants you to have His "dunamis" power. Dunamis is a Greek word that means or encompasses: power, ability, enablement, might, strength, miracle-working, etc. There are a number of places where dunamis is found in the Bible. Here we are focusing on receiving the Holy Spirit.

In Acts 1:4-5, Jesus commanded his apostles, "Do not depart from Jerusalem, but wait for the promise of the Father, of which you have heard from Me. For John baptized with water, but you shall be baptized with the Holy Spirit not many days from now." He later said to them in verse

8, "But you shall receive power (*dunamis*) when the Holy Spirit comes upon you. And you shall be My witnesses in Jerusalem, and in Judea and Samaria, and to the ends of the earth."

The apostles did what Jesus commanded them to do. In the book of Acts of the Bible, 120 people including the apostles, women and Mary, the mother of Jesus, were all together in the upper room waiting and praying. On the day of Pentecost, they experienced something quite different. They suddenly heard a sound from heaven likened unto a mighty rushing wind that filled the whole house. Acts 2:3 states, "There appeared to them tongues as of fire, being distributed and resting on each of them, and they were all filled with the Holy Spirit (*dunamis*) and began to speak in other tongues, as the Spirit enabled them to speak."

The Lord wants His believers to have this dunamis power. In these times, there will be many things that hit the land, but He wants us to lean on the Holy Spirit.

Take a moment and go to your place of prayer. Invite the Holy Spirit to be with you and ask Him for the *dunamis* of the Holy Spirit. Let Him fill you with His love, comfort, strength and dunamis power from head to toe. The Holy Spirit enables us to be bolder witnesses for Him. This is the time for greater evangelism. God is calling us to be witnesses in our hometowns, to other cities, nations, and the world. Do not fear of what others may think. The Greater One is inside of us now enabling us with might, authority and wonder-working powers. The Holy Spirit will partner with us. That's two!

I grew up in the Catholic faith and believe in the trinity of God, the Father, Jesus the Son and the Holy Spirit. However, I had never heard about the speaking in tongues which many refer to as the evidence of the Holy Spirit. I remember years ago coming home from a New Year's church celebration. For the six months prior to that service, I watched people pray and speak in tongues in a non-denominational church. I thought that it was quite strange. I thought to myself, "If that makes them happy, that's great. Keep on." I did not have any desire to speak in tongues. However, after being in church for several hours where the Spirit of God was moving heavily, my heart was melted that New Year's early morning. On my drive home, I spoke out loud to the Lord and said, "Lord, if you want me to have this speaking in tongues thing, I'll receive it." I left it alone and went on home singing.

The next day, I got up and went to the shower as always. I found that there was something different. I started speaking in tongues. It was coming up from my belly and out of me. It was so strange; it was just bubbling up. I knew this was an answer to the request I made driving home from church that morning. I also knew that this was real. Can I tell you that a few times during those six months, I tried to replicate "speaking in tongues" in the natural? After all, I had studied Spanish, Japanese, and Kiswahili. I thought I could "learn" and "duplicate" the tongues...but I could not.

What was coming up out of me was unique to me from what I heard from others, and it was coming up fast. I guess the Holy Spirit was waiting for me to open the door to Him, and now that I had, He was spilling over with joy. I have found that receiving this gift was one of the best things that ever happened in my life. It allows me to pray things that I didn't know and has helped build me up with power. Whenever I do not know what to pray in English, I pray in tongues. When I need that surge of power and strength, I especially pray in tongues. I've heard others say that you have to tarry for the Holy Spirit. That wasn't my experience. He is a gift; receive Him. Each person's experience is different.

It is time to walk with confidence. The dunamis of the Holy Spirit will empower you. Yield to the Holy Spirit. Rise up in your faith and expect miracles, signs, and wonders!

Before I close, I want to circle back to what I mentioned in the beginning. The words *due, dew, do, deux* are homonyms – same sound, different spellings. In this time, we must be intentional about using our mouths to make God-inspired declarations and prayers. Life and death are in the power of the tongue. Speak life over your dreams, purpose, family, church, and all that is connected to you. Regardless if you have a deep bass voice or a squeaky voice, we must be on one accord giving the Lord the honor which He is *due*. Bless His name. Every knee shall bow, and every tongue shall confess that Jesus Christ is Lord. According to

2 Timothy 2:12, "If we suffer, we shall also reign with Him: if we deny Him, He also will deny us."

It is my hope that you have accepted the gift of salvation through Jesus Christ and the dunamis power of the Holy Spirit. "And let us not be weary in well doing: for in due season we shall reap, if we faint not (Galatians 6:9).

I decree and declare that as you finished this book, you have entered into your Dü Season. It is your appointment to reign. For the record, let me say it a second time. This begins your:

Double blessings

double honor

double strength

double wealth

double-takes

double redemption

double peace

double doors

double streams

double contracts

double benefits

double surprises,

double joy

double results

double power!

To God be the glory for the marvelous things, He has, is, and will be doing in your lives. I'm expecting great testimonies! Please share them at www.sunarise.org or info@ sunarise.org .

Do List

Ask yourself, "What has God called me to do?" List it on the next page. Don't feel obligated to fill in every line. You can add to the list as the Lord gives to you in days, months, and years to come, or create one similar for yourself.

To Do	Start Date	Completion Date	Notes

PRAYER

Prayer

In 2 Chronicles 20:20, it states to believe the prophets and you shall prosper. God gives us His prophetic word through His mouthpieces to reinforce the Word of God, which is the Holy Bible. So, let's not be weary in doing well and contend for our prophetic words to come to pass. Let's go:

Father, thank You for being our Daddy, God. We thank You that we are Your children. We have no reservations coming to You because You are our loving Dad. We honor and reverence You, Abba Father. You are so special to us. Whenever we feel weary, we can come to You.

Lord, we are at a crossroads in this season, and many decisions have to be made. We see and hear what the world is saying. We see the promotion of fear and terror that is trying to cover the land. In accordance with 2 Timothy, You said that You have not given us a spirit of fear, but of power, love, and a sound mind. Lord, you state in 2 Chronicles 7:14, "If My people who are called by My name would humble themselves, and pray, and seek My face, and turn from their wicked ways; then will I hear from heaven, and will forgive their sin and will heal their land."

We come before You today for forgiveness and healing of the land. We know that there is so much more that You want for us as Your children. We hold tight to 2 Chronicles 20:20 which says to believe the prophets, and You shall prosper. No matter what we face at this moment, we do not throw away our confidence which has great recompense of reward. You said that You would keep us in perfect peace as we keep our minds stayed on You.

Lord, thank You for the ability to focus, concentrate, and meditate on whatsoever things are lovely and of a good report. We choose to focus on Your love and goodness towards us. Even with wars, rumors of war, famine, and natural disasters that seem to shake the world, we will be steadfast and immovable, abounding in You and Your Word. We can rest because of the confidence that You give us through Psalms 91. We are safe and secure under your wings.

Father, thank You for our *due* season. We thank you that everything that has been held up from past seasons will come to pass. We decree that every dream, project, blessing, finance, and land, that You have promised will come forth without further delay. We superimpose God's plan over every scheme, plot, and tactic of the enemy that has delayed our blessings. For every overdue promise, we thank you in advance for the double benefits, blessings, comfort, and joy coming forth. For You declared that this is the appointed time to favor us. We embrace Your word that said you will restore the years that the locust, cankerworm, caterpillar have taken from our lives. This is our Kairos time!

We thank You, God, that this is our *dew* season! This is our season of miracles, signs, and wonders! We thank You that even special miracles will be made manifest. We thank You that You will even have us to *do* in greater measure. For Your word says that greater works that we will *do*. We thank You that even in a season where there appears to be lack or famine, You will send down provision to sustain us until we reach our Goshen. Thank you, Daddy God for the double portion, inheritance, anointing, strength, peace, courage, creativity, blessings, and honor.

Father, we thank You that what our hands have been made to *do* will give You glory. We thank You for the businesses, creative ideas, witty inventions, books, videos, songs, jobs, recipes, and so much more that will sprout up from the dry places. Thank You for watering our grounds Lord to make provisions. Thank You for giving us sight to see what we couldn't see before. Thank You for giving us the enlightenment of our potential.

Thank You for opening our eyes of understanding and for giving us the power to declare Your will and Word in this season.

Genesis 26:12 says, "Then Isaac sowed in that land, and reaped in the same year a hundredfold; and the Lord blessed him." We embrace the supernatural blessings.

Lord, forgive us for anything that we have done that has not been pleasing to You. Forgive us where we did not steward our time and resources responsibly. Forgive us for delayed obedience. Create in us a clean heart and renew the right spirit within us.

Lead us not into temptation and deliver us from evil.

For You, Oh Lord, is the Kingdom, the power, the glory forever and ever. We bless You, King of Kings and Lord of Lords. In Jesus' name. Amen.

DECLARATIONS

Declarations

God does not want us to only be hearers of the Word. We must also be doers. Life and death are in the power of the tongue, so let's use our mouth to affirm and make these positive declarations:

I do acknowledge Jesus as my Lord, personal savior, and redeemer.

I do see myself worthy because my elder brother Jesus died for all of my shortcomings and sin.

I do see myself as the head.

I do see myself as the lender.

I do minister with fire.

I do everything with integrity and for the glory of God.

I do make an impact.

I do declare that by Jesus' stripes, I am healed.

I do have power, love, and a sound mind.

I do receive my double portion and more.

I do position myself to receive my double portion, honor, favor, and blessings.

I do confess my love to God. I am so in love with Him.

I do see my marriage as blessed and only speak positively about my spouse.

I do see my household as blessed, and I confess the shalom of God, love, and financial freedom as my portion.

I do cultivate powerful, prayerful, and positive friendships and family relationships.

I do show myself friendly.

I do have an eye to see and a hearing ear.

I do use my voice to shape my world.

I do boldly use my voice as a weapon to annihilate demonic forces and hindrances.

I do overcome by the blood of the Lamb and the word of my testimony.

I do have a great testimony, and I will share it to be a blessing to others.

I do hear God's Word, and the voice of a stranger I do not follow.

I do operate in immediate obedience to God's Word.

I do set healthy boundaries for my life to protect myself as a Kingdom asset.

I do overcome evil with good.

I do make a difference.

I do positively impact my community, city, state, nation, and the world with my prayers and actions.

I do have a voice and use it to build up others and myself.

I do have something to contribute to society.

I do see myself as handsome/beautiful.

I do spend quality time with God, myself, and my family.

I do listen for the still small voice of the Lord.

I do see the good in others, as well as in myself.

I do praise the Lord.

I do love.

I do forgive.

I do minister with fire.

I do help.

I do create.

I do help resuscitate and bring revival to others with the Word of God and encouragement.

I do listen.

I do laugh.

I do tithe.

I do exercise and protect my body, the personal temple of God.

I do make wise investments.

I do sow into others.

I do pray.

I do see the best in others.

I do give words of affirmation.

I do complete projects.

I do rest.

I do shift.

I do collaborate as the Spirit leads.

I do wash myself in the Word of God.

I do put on the whole armor of God daily.

I do create conducive atmospheres to house God's glory.

I do receive mantles that will be used in the marketplace and to help build God's Kingdom.

I do have an eagle-like vision.

I do discern the times and seasons as the sons of Issachar.

I do have good health, and I prosper as my soul prospers.

I do hold steadfast to the Word of God.

I do cast off shame.

I do put on the cloak of God's love.

I do press towards the mark of the prize of the high calling in Christ Jesus!

I do walk into God-ordained doors without fear.

I do recognize Jesus Christ as the author and finisher of my faith.

I do know that all things are working for my good.

I do make room for the Lord.

I do take the limits off of God and myself.

I do see and experience God's manifested blessings.

I do hold fast to what God says. He will do exceedingly and abundantly above all that I ask or think.

I do receive my *due*, *dew*, *do*, and *deux* season.

I do decree and declare this in Jesus' name!

About the Author

Marina Angelica Coryat

Marina Angelica Coryat is the Owner of Refined Communications, LLC. She is an innovative, strategic and results-driven business relations leader with extensive experience in public affairs and community relations in corporate, non-profit, and governmental arenas. She also serves as the Communications Director for Texas State Representative Senfronia Thompson. Marina has a solid track record to lead and inspire by positively creating strategies, developing programs and building strong relationships. Some of her experience has been for organizations such as Blue Cross and Blue Shield of Texas, McDonald's franchise owners, and the City of Houston. As a goal-oriented advocate of continuous improvement, she solves problems creatively to exceed expectations, generate revenue, minimize expenses, and contribute to overall company branding, growth, and morale. She was also a political candidate on the November 2019 ballot for Houston's City Council.

In addition to her work, Marina is a Lifetime Member and Ambassador of the Greater Houston Partnership. Her desire is to see individuals grow to their fullest potential and reach their destiny. This drives her passion for serving as an Advisory Board Member for both United Way's Career and Recovery Resources, Inc., and the Houston Area Urban League (HAUL). She is also the HAUL Fund Development Chair and was the Co-chair of HAUL's 49th Annual Equal Opportunity Day Gala.

In 2018, SunArise International Ministries was founded by Minister Marina Coryat in Houston, Texas. This ministry was founded to spread the gospel of Jesus Christ and bring healing. The foundational scripture for this ministry is Malachi 4:2 and supported by Isaiah 60:1.

Minister Marina Coryat is a member of the IMPACT Network Global under the leadership of Apostle John Eckhardt. She is a graduate of Kingdom School of Ministry headed by Dr. Cindy Trimm as well as a graduate of the School of the Prophets under the leadership of Apostle Debra Ford and Dr. Linda Calloway of Faith International Ministries who licensed her in ministry on April 23, 2007. Minister Coryat is currently a member of the Windsor Village Church Family under the leadership of Senior Pastor Kirbyjon Caldwell where she leads the 12 Noon Prayer Altar Team, serves on the Miracles and Healing Team, as well as the Deliverance Team. Additionally, she has served in various ministry capacities at Lakewood Church, Love Ministries Family Church, Shekinah Throne Room Worship Center, and St. Benedict Catholic Church.

Marina holds a Bachelors of Arts degree from Cornell University in Ithaca, New York. She is also a graduate of Leadership Houston, Trimm Institute for Global Leadership, as well as the Center for Houston's Future. She has received numerous awards including 2016 Top 30 Influential Women in Houston.

Contact Information

Marina Angelica Coryat

Emails:

marinacoryat@gmail.com

marinacoryat@refinedcommunications.net

marinacoryat@sunarise.org

Websites:

www.marinacoryat.com

www.sunarise.org

www.refinedcommunications.net

Social Media:

Facebook: @marinaacoryat

Twitter: @marinaacoryat

Instagram: @marinaacoryat

Periscope: @marinacoryat

Made in the USA
Columbia, SC
26 October 2020